Mental Mode

Why You Should Not Only Rely On Them And What To Do Instead

By

Joseph Fowler

FREE BONUS!

Free Thinking Cheat Sheet Reveals...

21 timeless thinking principles you need to know to upgrade your thinking and make smarter decisions (not knowing these may hinder you from having the success you'd like to have in life)

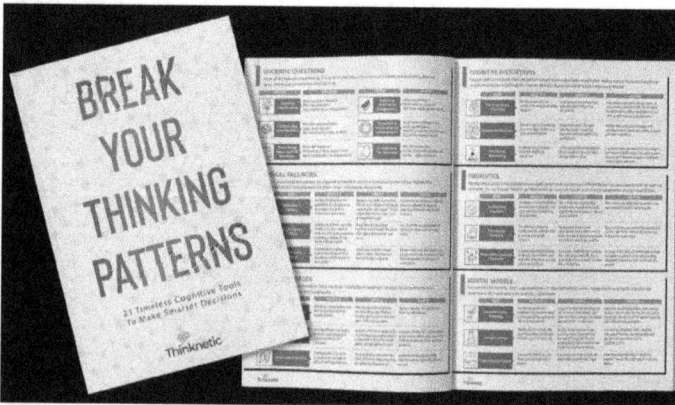

CLICK HERE TO DOWNLOAD FOR FREE!

Or go to www.thinknetic.net or
simply scan the code with your
camera

Table of Contents

Introduction

You may be aware of mental models. They are frameworks that shape your thinking, based on your background, values, goals, biases, education, and life experiences. They are quite useful in that they help you process information and make decisions without too many mental gymnastics. Yet they can be problematic when they trap you in a way of thinking that is no longer helpful in a specific situation or in life in general.

You may be terrified that your mental models are preventing you from making the right decisions to meet your goals and lead your best life. This is a legitimate problem, since mental model traps affect almost everyone. Fortunately, there is a way to retrain your brain to adopt new models and let go of unhelpful ones.

From breaking down biases that prevent you from trying something new, to helping you realize and overcome basic personality limitations, this book is your guide to overcoming the hurdles that mental models can create for you. Using real, concrete scientific evidence supported by credible studies, this book contains many examples of common mental models and how to work around them.

I know how it feels to be trapped in a mental model. As a psychologist, I see this happening all the time, to other people and to myself. Through careful research and experience, I have formulated workarounds for each mental model. My research has led me to understand that our minds make our lives and we make our minds, so I know that we all have the power to undo harmful mental models and get out of the mental traps that we can find ourselves in.

There are so many benefits to breaking free of your mind's own traps. The first is that you are able to become more creative, which helps you solve problems from new angles and aids you in work or art. The second is that you overcome fear that holds you back, making you a go-getter who stops at nothing for success. The third is that you become happier as you make your life happen. You stop defeating yourself. Finally, you will become a better spouse, parent, and leader, improving yourself in all areas of life. This is because you will find new ways to relate to people and you will have banished any biases that prevent you from forming close relationships. Your problem-solving abilities will get you many rewards in all areas of life, particularly work and family, since problems inevitably arise in everyone's lives.

If you wish to lead your best life, you must break down the mental model traps in your own mind. This book will help you reap all of the benefits of a free, unencumbered mind. I promise that by the end of this book, you will feel like a new person and you will have the tools to achieve success and solve problems.

But you don't want to wait any longer. You have already spent many years locked in the traps of mental models, defeating your own success and creating your own failures. You can make better decisions and become a happier person today if you start working on your own mind with the help of this book. So start reading now and see what a life free of mental model traps is like!

Chapter 1: When Your Mental Model Goes Wrong

Mental models are not bad things in and of themselves. In fact, they are incredibly useful for you in daily life. Sort of like a software system in a computer, mental models help your brain store and process information at a rapid speed, enabling you to make immediate decisions.

Think about when you meet a manipulative person. In the past, you met a similar person and had a bad experience. Your brain stored memories of that person and his traits, so you are better able to recognize them in this new acquaintance. You are able to make the snap decision: Steer clear of this guy!

Or think about when you are driving. You have been trained to stop at red lights and go at green lights. So when you see a red light, you stop and avoid an accident with oncoming traffic.

Mental models automate the decision-making process. This is great in many ways, as it removes the burden of gathering information and making decisions in situations where you need to think fast. It provides a framework that takes the guesswork out of life. There is nothing better than an instruction model on life, and that is exactly what a mental model is.

So when do mental models go wrong?

The truth is that the framework you have created in your mind may be wrong. Or it may be correct in certain situations, but not in every single situation. You rely on your mental models far too heavily, causing you to make decisions based on it even when it is not useful.

There is no single mental model from physics or engineering, for example, that provides a flawless explanation of the entire universe. Therefore, your brain can't possibly create a perfect mental model for all things in life, either. Maybe your mental model to steer clear of people who seem manipulative serves you well for the most part, except in business when such a manipulative person may be a very useful ally in making things happen.

The best mental models are the ideas with the most utility. They are broadly useful in daily life. But in certain situations where you must use logic and reasoning, you may let a mental model rob you of the ability to reason because you rely too heavily on old ways of thinking or biases. Instead of thinking, you let your mental model take over. Logic and rational choice theory are always better than relying on intuition, since intuition is often born of your mental models [1].

In new situations, you don't have all of the information. Thus, you must take some time to evaluate and make decisions based on new information. Mental models can interfere with that. Your brain likes to recognize patterns in things when no pattern may actually exist [2]. Hence, your brain assumes it knows more than it does and drives a choice that has no basis in reality. For instance, your brain may assume that someone is no good because he has the same hair as your ex and your brain erroneously thinks that same hairdo = same personality. This is a fake pattern.

The truth is that mental models are based on your own imagination and your unique perception of your experiences, which can mean that they are wildly inaccurate and at odds with reality. After all, reality is a subjective experience for each person. Therefore, you are relying heavily on something that is not even necessarily real, or that is built on misremembered facts, misunderstandings, and assumptions. Do you really want to base huge life decisions on something so fluid?

In my last book, *Mental Models and General Thinking Concepts,* you learned that mental models can come from your childhood experiences as well as universal cognitive biases. Your childhood experiences may not be congruent with your adult life; in fact, they are usually completely irrelevant as you change with age and life circumstances change with maturity. Furthermore, cognitive biases are helpful but often wrong, as they obscure reality and drive your thinking down a prescribed path. Hence, relying on these things can lead to some errors in judgment. The best way to avoid these errors is to take all of the facts and make a reasonable decision that is free of emotion.

That is why mental model traps are best avoided. Once you know that you are caught in a trap, it is not some horrifying reality. These traps have served you in at least some way. But to truly exercise good judgment and make wise decisions, you must remove these traps. Removing traps leaves your thinking clear and unimpeded. You can create a rationale for a better decision than previously. When it comes to all areas of life, this is obviously beneficial. Imagine what life could be like without tons of mental noise and bad decisions? Your finances would thrive, your family would be happy, and you would definitely feel better about yourself as a person.

Removing a mental model trap does not entail doing brain surgery. It does not even require that you permanently remove the trap. It simply means that you learn what traps look like and then recognize the signs of when you are operating within one. Then it is quite easy to adjust your thinking to something more helpful and logical. The traps will remain in your mind; they are a part of you. But as you avoid using them more and more, your brain builds new neural pathways to follow more helpful thinking tools in your mental toolbox, so it becomes more habitual to engage in stronger decision-making and problem-solving. It can take time, as long as sixty-six days [3], to create this habit; once you do, however, the effort will be removed from making wise choices and your life will improve with sounder logic.

Read on to learn about the different types of mental model traps that you probably engage in. These traps are harmful because of the way they impair your judgment and use cognitive biases that don't value facts and logic. Fortunately, once you learn about these traps, you can identify them as you engage in them and you can adjust your thinking accordingly.

How You Can Predict Traps

You are probably accustomed to making predictions about the future and estimates about unknown values. Life is always uncertain so you must make decisions without knowing all of the facts. However, there is a right way and a wrong way of dealing with unknowns. Here are a few traps that people tend to fall into when making decisions with unknown variables. By avoiding these traps, you can make wiser decisions based on logic, instead of universal mental models that often lead to failure.

When You Fall Into The Overconfidence Trap

You scored one hundred percent on a difficult exam. Now you are overconfident and you believe that you can ace every test in the semester without really trying. Imagine your shock when you fail the next test because you didn't study!

This is an example of overconfidence running afoul. When you engage in the mental model trap of overconfidence, you are overestimating your probability based on one or a few unusual successes. You blind yourself to reality, which is that your triumphs are built on a certain formula or even sheer good luck and your results are more likely to return to the mean in time.

Overconfidence is one example of a miscalibration of subjective probabilities. Instead of looking at the true probability of doing well, you assume that you will be the best. This prepares you for recklessness and disappointment in the end. Ego is always problematic, as it shrouds your judgment in a veil of contrived (and utterly useless) optimism. Avoiding ego is always wise when making life decisions.

Consider research that students who have low self-esteem tend to score better on tests [4]. Several studies have supported this finding. It is believed that students with low self-esteem about their knowledge actually apply themselves, think about questions more carefully, and study harder, which drives their scores up. Students with high self-esteem tend to assume they are the best, which causes them to misread their probabilities of scoring highly. They don't study and they don't think long and hard, causing them to bomb tests. Overconfidence drives this carelessness.

Overconfidence occurs in three distinct ways:

1. You overestimate your performance;
2. You overestimate your performance rated against the performance of others, believing that you are somehow better than other people;
3. You place exaggerated confidence in your own knowledge or abilities to predict the future, and you think that your beliefs are more accurate than they are.

As you engage in overconfidence, it can manifest in one of these three ways. And you may not be overconfident in every area of life, or in every situation. But even when it rears its head on occasion, overconfidence can create problems as you rely too heavily on yourself and fail to take your limitations or outside circumstances into account.

When you take a test and you assume that you know everything on the test, you may not see any need to study. This in turn makes you forget certain facts that surprise you on the test. This is when overestimating your knowledge is harmful.

As you audition for a sport, you may think that you are the best there is because you have been told that before by your parents or a biased coach. You think that you stack up better than other players who are also auditioning. You suffer quite an ego blow when you learn that other players were better than you. This is when you overestimate your performance against others. By abandoning the sense that you are superior and instead preparing for other people to be better than you, you are driven to try harder and practice better to be able to compete.

Finally, consider those people who insist that they can predict the stock market. In a study, most of those people failed to accurately predict the Dow Jones Industrial Average closing value [5]. Often, people were confident that the market would stay the way it currently is, hurting their chances of making more accurate predictions based on long-term trends and other important economic factors. Based on this evidence, it can be projected that in major business decisions that rely on accurate estimates of the stock market, twenty to thirty percent of executives would be dead wrong, which could cause significant harm to their companies [5].

Obviously, overconfidence can drive you to make some stupid decisions. But how do you know when you are in this trap? The main sign is when you feel absolutely sure of something. Since nothing in life is certain, this sense of certainty should alarm you. Ask yourself, "Why am I so sure of this?" Then consider that you are being overconfident and you should take some additional steps to protect yourself from making a careless decision.

This is not advice to actively cultivate low self-esteem and self-doubt. Numerous other studies have indicated that being confident is essential in life. The more confident you are, the more you succeed. But there is a big difference between confidence and overconfidence. When you are confident that you can pass a test, you use that confidence to motivate you to study because you know what you are capable of if you put in the work. Furthermore, if you don't do well, you don't let the low score destroy your self-esteem; rather, you learn from your mistakes and strive to do better because you know that you can score well eventually. When you are overconfident, you assume you will do well and you neglect studying. Then you are in for a rude awakening about your proficiency in the subject matter. Confidence is good, while overconfidence is dangerous.

The main takeaway is this: If you feel sure that you are right, that you are the best at something, or that you will succeed, think again. Just because you are an expert in a field or you have done well at something before does not mean that you will succeed or be right every time. The statistical probability that you will fail is still fifty percent every time you do something or make a prediction, regardless of past successes. It never hurts to study, practice, or otherwise work on your skills hard all of the time to increase your chances of success and correctness in more situations. It also never hurts to doubt your initial gut judgment and perform some research into the facts before basing a decision on what you assume to be true. Let confidence drive you to do better. Avoid overconfidence at all costs.

The Prudence Trap

Opposite of overconfidence, some people choose to be overly prudent. Hence, they avoid necessary risks and miss great opportunities. They let fear of failure or risk drive their choices. This trap is caused by a disproportionate trust placed in the possibility of lower estimates and failure.

Back to the stock market, you may underestimate how much a stock can grow, so you bail on it the minute there is a sign of trouble. Or you may overestimate your chance of failure when you open your own restaurant, so you never make that dream come true. Perhaps you overestimate the likelihood that you will die in a plane crash, so you refuse to take your dream trip to the Bahamas and you never get to experience that beautiful place for yourself.

Being overly prudent is never good. While it is always wise to investigate your options and be cautious, don't rely too much on your gut sense of probability. The odds of something bad happening are almost always equal to the odds of something good happening. Odds can vary according to situations, so get a better sense of your true odds through research before you assume the worst.

Reframe your fears. Instead of focusing on potential loss, consider potential gain. Some risks are worth taking. If your potential gains are much greater than potential losses, take the risk. Furthermore, it is possible to mitigate most potential losses. You can create a financial safety net for if your restaurant fails, for example. By creating a safety net, you can pad yourself against loss and make a risk even more worthwhile. The wisdom "Prepare for the worst, hope for the best" is a wise attitude to take in life and guard against both the overconfidence and over-prudence traps.

Recallability Trap

The idea that is the most dramatic stands out more in your mind. The event that happened recently is more relevant than events from farther back in time. The information that is simplest and thus easiest to recall is more readily available to retrieve from your memory than more complex information.

Your brain likes to conserve energy as much as possible. Thus, you don't like mining your subconscious for ideas, memories, and facts. You instead rely on that which is most recallable. The issue with this is that the most recallable information may not be the most relevant information.

Think about when you took a trip to Costa Rica. It was all nice...until you sustained a surfing injury. That last experience was pretty negative and dramatic, so it remains on the forefront of your mind. When you have to pick a vacation destination again, you might refuse to go back to Costa Rica, no matter how nice it was besides the mishap.

Or consider when two people make presentations for marketing ideas. The first person actually has the most ingenious idea that really will work. The second person uses a live model and loud music with her presentation, however, so it stands out as more recallable. You forget all about the first person's great idea and go with her shoddier idea just because you can recall it better.

These are just examples of how the recallability trap fails you. When you focus on just one thing that stands out in your mind, you miss all of the rest.

Having more facts in mind expands your toolbox and leaves you more prepared for decisions.

Circle Of Competence

Do you operate from a place of competence or from a place of ego? Let me elaborate a little more. When faced with a challenge, do you delve into your skills and find the best way to overcome that challenge using what you know? Are you willing to outsource work and avoid taking on challenges that you don't have the skillset to solve? Or do you take on anything and everything and refuse to get help, insisting that you are good at anything you do?

Delving into your skills and finding solutions illustrates the circle of competence [6]. But taking on tasks you are not qualified for and refusing to get help illustrates using ego. When you use your circle of competence, you are employing a bit of humility and acknowledging that you don't everything about everything. You stick to your specific skillset.

Throughout life, we become very competent in certain areas. But we just don't have the means to be competent in all areas. We are strong sometimes, and weak sometimes. I am strong in social sciences, such as psychology and sociology, but I am clueless when it comes to calculus and physics, for instance. The fact I am willing to admit that enables me to avoid taking on tasks and jobs that require these upper level math skills, where I would completely fail.

To use your circle of competence, you are escaping the mental model trap of ego. You are analyzing your skills and seeing where you are competent and incompetent. Thus, you are able to draw from your strengths, and designate tasks you are weak in to other people who are strong in them. This makes for a good person, a good leader, and a good worker.

Warren Buffett is a staunch believer of utilizing the circle of competence. He encourages investors to only stay within their areas of expertise. Imagine investing in tech companies when you have no tech knowledge – how do you know if a company has the potential to be successful if you aren't a tech guy yourself? But this concept goes far beyond investing and applies to every part of life. In work, you can take on things that you can do well and designate tasks to other teammates that you can't do well. In marriage, you can solve the problems and conflicts that you know how to solve, and employ a third party such as a couples counselor when you come up against issues you can't address. You may also let your spouse handle the finances if you are not so good with money and do the dishes because your spouse can't seem to get them clean enough.

Furthermore, you can use the circle of competence to challenge yourself to learn more about many things. The more you know, the better your skillset is. Reality is multidisciplinary – psychology, physics, biology, mathematics, and so much more. The more knowledge you possess from all disciplines, the richer your mental toolbox is, and the larger your circle of competence. You are less inclined towards overconfidence, however, because you know that no one knows everything about everything. When you are unsure, you don't let pride cloud your judgment as you seek help from reputable sources.

To grow your mental toolbox, I urge you to dedicate yourself to a life of learning. You are never too old to learn. As you broaden your mental toolbox, you will be able to tackle more challenges and tasks in life. Always study things that you are not comfortable with or don't enjoy, because even those bits of knowledge can enrich your toolbox. I am horrible at math but I still try to learn what I can in case I ever have to use it. For example, I found that understanding basic physics helps me understand psychology better, because I now know from physics that two opposite things can be equally true and that often applies to psychology as well.

Don't be afraid to learn about things that you don't agree with, so that you can become more balanced in your opinions and more educated about your opponents. For example, if you are firmly against abortion, you will not make a very argument against it by simply spouting out your feelings about the matter. Researching abortion and why people do it can help you become a more informed pro-life activist and build better arguments that actually make sense in the real-world context. The opposite is equally true if you are pro-choice.

More knowledge and skills will never let you down. Neither will becoming familiar with opinions and ideals incongruent with your own. The more you know about all areas of life, the more you are able to competently address the myriad of problems and challenges life has in store for you.

When You Use Narrow Thinking

Narrow thinking will get you into hot water every time. When you are looking at life through a narrow lens, you are preventing yourself from seeing every possibility and differentiation. Thus, you are bound to make a mistake in judgment.

Narrow thinking is supported by a few main cognitive biases that people engage in. The first is confirmation bias, wherein people decide they hold a belief and then they look for confirmation in everything [2]. They never consider that they may be wrong and they choose to block out or disprove every bit of evidence that disproves their beliefs in what is called disconfirmation bias [2]. Furthermore, when new facts are irrefutable, they tend to ignore these facts in what is called the ostrich effect [2]. Like ostriches burying their heads in the sand, people hope that unpleasant reality can go away if they just don't look at it.

Narrow thinking can also be reinforced by the tendency people have to sort things into neat categories, ignoring the reality that nothing is so black and white [2]. For instance, a lot of people will sort people into good and bad. Then they are shocked when a supposed good person does something wrong or when a supposed bad person is capable of kindness and reformation. They ignore the reality that people are always a blend of good and bad.

To break out of the habit of narrow thinking, you must stop dismissing reality that you don't like and sorting things into neat categories. Consider that you may be wrong and you should investigate other options to find what speaks truth to you. Consider that there is more to life than two categories and some things fall into a gray area.

It is essential to avoid looking for the correct answer and instead find alternative answers. If you are wrestling between two diametrically opposed ideas, you are probably employing narrow thinking. There is probably a solution that blends elements from both opposing ideas, if you would look at life through a wider lens.

A good example is how people in the United States tend to sort themselves into two categories, Republican or Democrat. Both political systems have their merits and demerits and both parties tend to dismiss the other's good ideas about healthcare reform just because they perceive each other as the enemy. This makes it impossible to ever compromise. The American healthcare crisis could be solved if both parties stopped insisting on the correctness of their own approaches and instead considered how to blend their approaches and borrow strengths from each other's ideas to create a truly unique healthcare system that covers all bases. People are often too narrow in their thinking and too black and white in their viewpoints to allow such a blending of diametrically opposed ideas, unfortunately. This is why third parties and independent candidates never quite succeed.

For a more personal example, consider when you are debating between moving into a large house that you can't afford or a small house that doesn't meet all of your space needs. Either decision has so many trade-offs that you can't pinpoint the best move. Did you consider that you should not move into either house, but instead find another house that is both bigger and more affordable? Have you tried shopping in other areas of the city to find the best option? By considering alternatives, you don't have to select the lesser of two evils or compromise on something important to your values.

Often, when you can't decide on something, you are overlooking an important part of the equation by using narrow thinking. Being creative entails finding new ways to approach a problem that you never considered before. Having knowledge in lots of disciplines and entertaining opinions incongruent to your deeply held beliefs can help you become flexible and creative enough to accomplish this.

It is far better to learn as much as you can to expand your mental toolbox. As you add tools to this toolbox, you have more creative and varied ways of handling problems. You can locate the proper way to handle a problem more easily and make better decisions based on your wide range of knowledge. Consider the example of how Richard Feynman learned a unique way of solving differential equations in calculus and was able to tackle problems that his cohorts could not because of this knowledge. He was not smarter than everybody else; he was more open-minded to creative solutions. Hence, he won the Nobel Prize in 1965. If you bother to learn things different from what everyone else knows, and even different from what you already know, you can solve more problems than other people and your knowledge becomes that much more useful.

How You Fall For Anchoring And Framing

Would you believe that a lot of your decisions are trapped by things called anchors and frames? These traps may be deliberately or accidentally set up by others, but they constrict your thinking, keeping you from the best decision or more accurate prediction. By learning to identify these two traps, you can successfully free your thinking and become more independent and accurate in your decisions.

Anchoring

An anchor weighs down your thinking significantly by imposing an upper or lower limit on your estimations. Hence, your estimate becomes capped or boxed in some way. You can't make the right decision with this arbitrary limitation in place.

Let's explore how anchoring works in real life. If you are negotiating your salary at a new job, the initial offer may be $35,000. You think that you are worth at least $70,000, but this $35,000 offer imposes an anchor. You become scared to ask for much higher than $35,000 because you assume that you will be declined, so you only ask for $45,000. Thus, you willingly take a lower salary all because of an anchor your boss set in your mind.

However, you could beat this anchor by researching average salaries in your field. The information you learn can make you more confident about the salary you deserve and how much you can realistically expect to get paid at any organization in your career, so you negotiate something fairer.

Or consider when you're purchasing a used car. The car is ludicrously overpriced at $20,000 but you don't know its actual worth, so you let $20,000 sway your offer. You are not eager to go too far from that initial price when making an offer. The car dealership thus gets a lot of extra money out of you.

However, you can beat that anchor by doing research. When you happen to know the value of the car is only $13,000, you have another more accurate anchor set in your mind and you are able to make a more informed offer. Whether or not the dealership accepts it is impossible to predict, but at least you don't get ripped off.

When you see any number or value, understand that that makes an anchor in your mind. To work around the anchor, do your research. Find out the appropriate value to create a more accurate anchor in your mind. Do not accept anchors from people who set them arbitrarily. Add research to your mental toolbox. Kelley Blue Book is a great mental tool for buying cars; Glassdoor is a great tool for determining salaries; and so on.

Also, realize that most things in life are somehow anchored. When you don't have much evidence, other people will advertently or inadvertently take advantage of that. For example, it has been determined that a BMI below 25 is associated with fewer health problems. But BMI does not take things into account like muscle mass, so you may feel guilty and even stressed that you are over 25 when really your risk of health problems is not any higher because your body fat is still low. You wrap your dietary decisions and even your self-esteem around this arbitrary BMI value that was set by perceived nutrition experts and doctors. This clouds your sense of reality.

Start to break free of these anchors that exist everywhere by considering what looks and feels best to you, regardless of what other so-called experts say. Don't even let popular science bend your decisions, since popular science is often fluid and changes from one day to the next; case in point is how eggs were once considered bad for you a decade ago but now they're supposedly good for you, so you might wonder which truth is the correct one.

You have the power to set up your own reality, but you tend to rely too much on the anchors created by other people.

Framing

Framing is as entrapping as anchoring, but it tends to use linguistical variations to set traps on thinking rather than numbers. Basically, the way something is phrased can obscure its true meaning. Your decisions can be influenced by whether or not something sounds good, regardless of what it actually implies.

To cope with framing, consider when something seems obvious to you, such as a gut decision. Now try reframing the problem in various ways to see if your get decision changes. Maybe try rephrasing the same question ten different ways to find the most complete answer, for example.

Why You Are Resistant To Change

Humans are quite stubborn. Change involves a lot of uncertainty, which is scary. We often don't want to take risks. So, we resist change as best we can. This results in missed opportunities or hanging onto things and situations that make us miserable.

What if you are trapped in an abusive marriage? While you know that the marriage is bad, you are even more scared of moving and having no money and being alone, so you stay. You don't want to waste the time already invested in the marriage or change the status quo. What you are doing is staying in a dangerous, explosive situation in order to maintain the status-quo and avoid sunk costs.

These are the two main fallacious mental model traps that prevent you from making beneficial change. To keep from being stuck, particularly in harmful situations, you should learn to avoid these traps at all costs.

When You Keep The Status Quo

People are biased to maintain the status quo, or the perceived normalcy of something. As humans are naturally resistant to change, maintaining the status quo can be a hidden motive behind many decisions. Acting in ways that upset the ways things already are is why problems go unsolved for decades and organizations fade into obsoleteness as they don't bother staying relevant with evolving trends.

However, it is clear from evidence that the people and organizations most open to change tend to succeed more and last longer than those that are not. Maintaining the status quo is seldom a good idea. Change can provide the basis for survival.

If you run a business and you notice that your current form of advertising is not yielding many results, you might be tempted to hold out and see if it changes.

But you continue to waste money on the same unsuccessful advertising methods. The result is lost money and less revenue. By going against the status quo, you can find a new means of advertising that works better.

Often, people do things just because that is the way things have always been done. For example, the first online newspapers were created just like print papers and the first cars looked just like horse-drawn carriages. Finding more efficient designs for something or more efficient ways of doing tasks can break open amazing results. Look at the things you do and ask if there is a more efficient system. Don't just do things because that's the way you learned to do them or because other people do things that way.

Consider if the status quo is problematic or actually fine the way it is. Don't fix things that aren't broken. But if something is broken, then fixing it is ideal. Always seek to streamline systems and fix processes that are inefficient or unsuccessful. Obviously, the status quo is not working, so changing it is not going to be terrible.

When You Fall For The Sunk Cost Fallacy

This fallacy is another way that people elaborately construct their thinking and decisions to avoid change. In this fallacy, you may not let a stock go that is losing money because you have already invested so much money into it and you don't want to waste anything. Or you may not want to get divorced because you have invested twenty-five years into a marriage, even though neither of you are happy and both of you want something different. Or you refuse to move from an old house that has become a money pit since you have already spent hundreds of thousands renovating it.

When you perceive that you have already spent so much time, money, effort, or resources on something, you resist the idea of letting it go. You tend to hold onto some object, person, or idea to avoid the pain of loss and the sense that you have wasted anything. You continue to let this thing you are clinging to drain you further, instead of realizing that it no longer serves you and moving onto something that does serve you.

If something is costing you more than it is worth or if something is no longer making you happy, you should not consider what you have wasted on it. Instead, consider how it served you for a time and was worth what you put into it. By cutting it loose, you can now move on to something more beneficial.

This hardly means that you should jump ship on a relationship at the first sign of trouble or sell your house the minute the roof springs a leak. Many things are worth fixing and keeping. But if something becomes so burdensome that it costs you far more than it gives you, it may be time to let it go. Weigh the costs of something versus the benefits to make a logical decision about what to do. Don't let the past influence these decisions.

Chapter 2: How Do You Break The Barriers?

As you can see from the last chapter, your mental model traps erect barriers in your mind to the best decisions and the most effective solutions. How can you break down these barriers and make better decisions and solve more problems in life? How can you become the best version of yourself possible without mental model traps standing in the way?

The solution to barriers is not always easy or convenient. But it is essential to going far in life and being happier with your decisions. By building more high-quality mental models, you can recognize when you are using a mental model that is trapping you and then switch to a more helpful model with greater utility that you know to fit the situation at hand. You can avoid bad decisions and the experience of being stuck in life. You can achieve things you never thought possible before.

Where Your Mental Models Tend To Go Wrong

While you learned about lots of mental model traps in the previous chapter, now let's explore how these traps influence your performance and experience in different areas of life and common life situations. Then, we will delve into alternative ways of thinking that lead to better outcomes.

A mental model sets an expectation (possibly false or unreasonable) for reality. You believe you will encounter what your mind predicts. Yet when it doesn't happen, you are left reeling, uncertain of how to proceed. It is a cruel joke that we experience this, since our mental models are based on our experiences and feelings and not probable fact. Plus, we seldom have a full picture of reality or a system since it is too large for our brains to comprehend, so we often miss critical things that sway outcomes. We are typically blindsided by reality, when we are so sure that our predictions are just dead-on.

Thus, mental models create some pretty significant barriers in our minds. They construct a reality that may not be accurate – at all. Thus, breaking down these barriers is imperative to making wise choices and solving problems correctly.

What You Can Do About It

To overcome these blind spots that poorly constructed mental models create in life, there are a few things that we can do to limit the use of mental models and get our thinking out of traps. Following are some strategies to work around mental models and their traps.

Build Yourself Concept Maps

A concept map can guide you to the reasonable conclusion, regardless of your mental models. As you jot down different ideas and facts, you cannot forget them or ignore them anymore [7]. Everything lays before you. Furthermore, concept maps help you break things down into important points and less important points [7].

At the very pinnacle of the map, you have your main point or subject. This could be some decision you are grappling with – "Moving" or "Taking a new job." Or, you could summarize a problem – "Boosting test scores" or "Making More Money." You don't want to add details to the point. Just a simple phrase that sums up the basic premise will do.

Next, find the key concepts related to the main idea. If you are deliberating a move, you could consider the key concepts of place, time, cost, and even basic pros and cons to moving. Again, keep the key concepts short and sweet without tons of detail.

Now you can start to get more minute with each additional step. Under cost, you can list things such as the cost of a U-Haul, the deposit on a new rental, etc. You might add something in there like, "How will

I afford this?" Then, under that question, you can list some ideas for raising or saving money to afford this. Do this for every concept, breaking it down into the most minute details you can think of.

The last part is connecting words and phrases that are related. The timing of your move may relate strongly to the cost. You can only move when you have the costs covered. So, you might link the two.

Doing this can be quite therapeutic. It organizes your thoughts and presents them simply. It helps you see ideas that don't even fit into the decision, so you can stop obsessing over them.

Employ First Principles Reasoning

What principles in a logical problem come first and foremost? Which ones can be ignored or abandoned because they really are not important? With first principles thinking, you break things down to the simple core truth and you go from there [8].

A great example is when I wanted to leave my job. I knew that I was unhappy, but I kept letting various doubts cloud my judgement. "What if a new job doesn't pan out? What if I get a bad reference? What if my boss gets angry when I give him my resignation?" All of these worries and more swirled through my head. I bet you know what that feels like because you have probably done the same thing yourself.

Eventually, I got sick of going back and forth and I knew I couldn't take another year at my job. I broke it down to the first principle – I wanted to quit! So, I figured out each problem that quitting posed and I figured out how to mitigate each problem to come out on top. By the end of the year, I was in a new position and much more satisfied with my life. And my boss wasn't even that mad when I resigned and gave me an excellent reference! I was so scared of something that didn't even happen. I was inspissating the situation in my own mind, supplementing it with my own imagination, and as a result I was blocking my path to success and happiness.

When you break something down to the simplest truth, you remove a lot of excess noise that confuses you and makes the obvious answer unclear. You let little worries, imagined worst-case scenarios, and the like cloud your judgment. You also tend to accept things as true that are not necessarily true.

Understand that life is different for you than anyone else. Your truths may not be true for anyone else and that's OK. It does not mean you are doing anything wrong. When you try to reason by analogy and apply what someone else did to your own life with slight variation, you will often miss some important fact and do something that doesn't really work for you. Finding your own unique truths and solutions is always imperative.

So, start by breaking a situation into its core pieces. In my example, I wanted to quit but I was scared of consequences.

Identify your vision or goal. It must be as specific as possible. Mine was that I wanted a job I could be happy in.

List every obstacle, real or imagined. My obstacles included finding a new job, posting my resume without getting terminated at my current position, talking to my boss to resign, and getting a good reference.

Look at your current assumptions about the obstacles. Then ask if they are real or not. Test them out. I assumed my boss would get angry and refuse to give me a good reference, thus making it hard to get a new job. But when I actually worked up the nerve to speak to him, I found out he was not angry at all. By resigning in a professional manner, nothing bad happened. I was banking everything on an assumption about another person, which I know not to do!

Find the most reasonable and creative solution. Dare to do something unprecedented. My solution was to talk to my boss face to face and explore my options. This was very difficult for me, but it was a creative solution, one I would have never thought of on my own. It worked out in my favor.

Use First- And Second-Order Thinking

First order thinking is where you make a snap decision to address a problem in the short-term. Meanwhile, you inadvertently create more long-term problems [9]. On the other hand, second-order thinking dives in a bit deeper and ponders the far-reaching consequences of each decision to determine the best one overall.

When I write about this, I think of my niece and a spectacular mistake she made. She took a title loan on a car and became horrified when the 150% interest rate made her few hundred dollars blossom into thousands in a few months' time. So, she traded her car in for another one that was much more expensive, taking on a car loan that she really couldn't afford. Since she couldn't make title loan payments, she definitely couldn't make these more expensive car payments. But since the car dealership paid off her title loan for her, she considered it to be a good decision. Fast forward eight months and she was facing her first car repossession. She did not have another car for years because of the cycle of bad debt she got trapped in. This catastrophic decision-making is an example of a time when second-order thinking really needs to be used.

Absolutely never seize on the first, most obvious, and simplest choice. More testing and thinking are always required. Really consider the long-term implications.

Anything that fixes the short-term without addressing the long-term is a bad idea.

We love instant gratification [10]. It is just human nature to want something solved right now and right here. Learning to stave off instant gratification for a long-term reward is a skill that you must develop over time. It hurts almost physically because you feel as if you are depriving yourself, but when you reap the long-term rewards, you are grateful you made such a smart choice.

You Should Ask Why Five Times

When you are facing a problem, it can seem confusing or complicated because of all of the various factors present. Yet when you break it down by asking the question, "Why?" you can simplify matters so much that the solution becomes apparent.

Many people make the mistake of slapping a Band-

Aid on problems, so to speak [11]. Instead of addressing the real root of the problem, they solve the symptoms of the problem. The result is that the problem persists. By asking why, you can pare the problem down to its root. When you address the root, you clear up the problem for good.

Usually, it is a human factor that leads to the problem. Human factors can be the simplest to address because they are more under your control than, say, a weather factor. For example, if you ask why you're not doing well in a tennis game, you may blame the weather in a self-serving bias which is totally out of your control, or you may actually realize what you are doing wrong and correct it. It is easy to rectify what you are doing wrong if you honestly identify the problem at hand. Asking why can get you to that point.

Here is 5 why's in action:

1. Why do I want to move? Because I want to explore

a new place.

2. Why do I want to explore a new place? Because I feel I might be limited where I am now.

3. Why do you think you will be trapped in your same home? I can't explore where I am. I want to try new things. New experiences shape life, right?

4. Why can't you go on day trips and explore from your new home? That's a good question.... Maybe I could explore the world around me without having to move.

5. Why don't you explore new places now? There is no reason I don't. So I guess I will! Let me try that before I commit to a big move.

You Can Use A Fishbone Analysis

Asking five why's is great in some situations. But it tends to offer only one-dimensional answers following a certain track of thinking. To expand your thinking and become more creative, you can use a fishbone analysis that considers several alternatives and leaves room for more ideas as they occur to you

[12].

Like a concept map, a fishbone analysis is a visual map of cause and effect. You start by creating the head of the fish, a basic summary of the problem you are facing. For instance, "Web servers are down at work."

Next, draw a straight line from the head to the left, creating the backbone. Write down four possible causes of this issue that you can think of. Add more when evidence comes to light.

Now, draw a bone, an angled arrow coming up or down off the backbone. List four possible solutions to each possible cause of the problem in front of the possible cause. Go through them and check them off as you complete them.

Chapter 3: Breaking Your Mental Models Down

In my last book, *Mental Models and General Thinking Concepts,* I covered many common mental models. These models are often based on biases or heuristics that streamline, and also limit, decisions. Thus, it is best to recognize these in your thinking and work around them. In this chapter, I will show you the common mental models and how to break them down for better decisions.

Confirmation Bias

You see this one all of the time in politics. People who deny climate change will twist scientific observations on the Earth to fit their agenda, while those who believe in climate change will twist the facts the other way. No one really knows who is right, but a lot of people think that they are right.

You can identify this bias when you find yourself

mining studies or news for proof of your beliefs. When you have to stretch facts to fit a belief, you are also engaging in this bias. Furthermore, you are engaging in it when you deliberately don't listen to someone and just pay attention to the one or two things someone says that seem to support your beliefs.

It is best to clear your mind of your beliefs before you take in new facts. Have the goal of learning something new. Read or listen to the facts with equal attention. Then decide what you want to do with them. You cannot dismiss certain facts or hype up other ones; you must treat all facts with equal weight.

Disconfirmation Bias

This is where you disconfirm the things you don't believe to support your confirmation bias. The second you hear something you don't agree with, you put on the brakes and find some way to dismiss the idea or disprove it just to keep your own beliefs intact [13].

The problem with this is pretty clear. What if you are wrong in an idea or belief? By refusing to change your belief, you make incorrect decisions that land you in hot water. You don't allow other people or facts to change your mind where necessary.

It is not good to constantly switch beliefs. You need some solid ground to start from. That is why it is OK to be stubborn about certain beliefs. But imagine if you're an investor and you believe the stock market will soar this year and instead a recession is happening. You ignore the evidence and don't play the market as you should because you are too busy holding onto your incorrect prediction. What happens? Well, you lose all of your money. When a belief you have endangers you or is far too wrong to ever mesh with reality, then you would be wise to change it.

You can identify this when you read or listen to something and then deny all of the facts in it except the few that support your beliefs. You can also identify it when you ignore facts or skim over them to find things that do support what you believe. When you dismiss an entire conversation or article because it doesn't match your beliefs, you are engaging in this bias.

Backfire Effect

Have you ever attempted to convince someone to your way of thinking? Chances are, it backfired in your face. Related strongly to confirmation bias, the backfire effect is where you cannot change anyone's minds [13]. In fact, if you challenge people in what they believe, people will actually hold onto their beliefs even harder, as a way to mitigate the threat of being wrong.

In most cases, as you attempt to persuade or dissuade

someone, know that you are setting yourself up for failure. Ask yourself, "Does it really matter if I convince this person of a fact?" Pick your battles and conserve energy for more useful pursuits.

When you do really need to convince someone of something, you can employ some of the tactics covered in *How to Make Friends and Influence People* by Dale Carnegie. This book has excellent strategies that work with the human mind to prove a point, such as dramatizing your ideas and avoiding arguments.

Self-Serving Bias

When you lose a game, you blame the weather or an unfair coach. When you win, you attribute it to your finesse and skill at the sport. This is self-serving bias [13]. It is created to protect your ego. However, it blinds you to important information that can help you grow and learn.

When you find yourself blaming outside circumstances, take a moment to reflect on what you did wrong. This allows you to identify holes in your performance that you can repair to be more successful in the future. So, ponder how you played poorly so that you can play better next time.

On the other hand, when you do remarkably well at something, ask yourself if any outside circumstances helped you achieve your success. That way, you can replicate those conditions to repeat success in the future. If you played really well, was it because of a certain way your coach had you practice or a certain meal you ate?

Fundamental Attribution Error

When your co-worker makes a mistake, you blame it on his innate laziness and poor work ethic. Yet when he succeeds, you believe that his success is based on luck or some other outside factor. In fundamental attribution error, you attribute results to the wrong things [13].

This error is most destructive in relationships, where you blame a person for everything and never consider there were factors beyond his or her control. That is why you should take a moment to think before you blame someone you love or someone you work with and damage the relationship. Most things are not the direct result of someone's personality, but rather a combination of personality and outside factors.

Hindsight Bias

After the 2008 real estate crisis, a lot of market experts swore that they knew it was coming. But if so many people knew the crash was coming, why did no one do anything about it? The hindsight bias is where you learn information and then assume that you had always known it all along [13]. Then you beat yourself up for not predicting something that you now think of as inevitable.

When you find yourself thinking, "I should have known!" or "Why didn't I do [blank]? It was so obvious I needed to do that," you are engaging in hindsight bias. Remember that you did not always have the information that you do now.

Dunning-Kruger Effect

Once I heard a friend criticize some photos I did. He said, "I used to have a lot of photos taken of me when I was skateboarding. I know a lot about photography." I knew he was not an expert in photography, especially considering that he was a model, not a photographer. I safely dismissed his criticism and relied more on the feedback of an actual professional.

In the Dunning-Kruger Effect, people insist that they

are experts in subjects that they know little about [13]. By having only a small window of knowledge, their view is far too simplistic and it convinces them that they know everything about the subject. On the other hand, a true expert knows that he doesn't know everything so he is far humbler in his approach to any subject. If you are positive that you know everything about something, think again. You are probably engaging in this mental model trap and making yourself look like an idiot! I always recommend learning more about each field and fact-checking before you spout something as true.

Reciprocity Model

When someone does you a solid, you feel obligated to return the favor. When a business gives you a free sample, you feel obligated to sign up for the service or buy the product. These are examples of reciprocity [14]. Often, you let this principle manipulate your thinking, even if you should not.

The minute you feel some sort of obligation, be wary of why. You are not obligated to anything just because someone gave you a free sample or a piece of candy. Furthermore, when someone offers to do you a favor, bear in mind that this person wants you to pay it back in some way, even if he claims he doesn't. Quite seldom do people do things out of altruism.

Occam's Razor

It is stated in conventional wisdom that the simplest answer is the best one. The more assumptions you have to make, the less likely something is true [13]. But is that really true? With so many parts of life falling into gray areas, how can we be certain that a simple answer will suffice?

Assumptions are always bad. They are guesses, based on limited evidence, that we believe to be true. Operating on assumptions sets us up to be wrong. When you assume something, do more research to find out if your assumption is right or wrong. If you assume that someone is mad at you, ask him or her before believing it.

When you have two or more answers, don't just go with the simplest one. That one may be the correct answer, but you don't really know that. You must test all possible answers and look for more evidence.

Optimism/Pessimism Bias

Depending on your mood, your view of the future is slanted toward optimism or pessimism. If you are in a great mood, you might look optimistically on a merger and insist that it's a great idea without doing a deeper analysis. Meanwhile, if you are in a bad mood, you will see the problems associated with the merger more than the benefits and so you avoid making a good decision. This is the optimism/pessimism bias at work [13].

When you get a sense for a decision, consider that fact-checking and running a cost-benefit analysis is still in order. You don't want to let your emotions sway the decision. Facts remain solid while emotions are fluid, so rely on the facts.

Negativity Bias

When you think that the negative consequences of a decision are so much more significant than the positive ones, you tend to place more weight on the negative ones [13]. This is the negativity bias. It blinds you to potential benefits and pros because you convince yourself that the cons are so much huger. An example is when you are pondering a move to another city and you let the fear of being lonely outweigh the wider career options and greater amount of things to do. You end up not moving, even if the move was indeed in your best interest.

The minute you find yourself circling back to the

same "What if?" or "But...this might happen," write down that central worry. Ask yourself if the worry is even realistic or simply your imagination. Then ask if the worry is big enough to outweigh other benefits. A pros and cons list can be helpful in this situation, as well.

Hanlon's Razor

When your partner doesn't text you back, you assume he or she is angry with you. When your co-worker doesn't send you the papers you requested, you assume he is being malicious and trying to get you in trouble at work. Never attribute to malice what can be attributed to stupidity: this is Hanlon's Razor [13].

Before you take something personally, consider that there is probably a more likely explanation for behavior. Seldom do people do things out of spite. There is probably a better answer. Find it before you become angry and accuse something of malice.

Think about what you would have done in their shoes. Look at the circumstances and see if there is a cause for someone's actions. Also, consider what someone may be going through. Finally, assume the goodwill of the other person, as few people are intentionally mean or destructive.

Forer Effect

When you don't understand something, you try to fill in the blanks with ideas that make intuitive sense to you but don't have any evidence. You see this all of the time in psychology. A guy keeps dating cruel women and the psychologist doesn't know his full background, so he proposes the guy had a bad relationship with his mother.

You also see it in school. A kid doesn't understand part of his science text about how frogs metamorphosize, so he fills in the blanks with totally false information and skips important steps in the process.

When you draw a blank and decide to fill it in with the most logical or intuitive answer, stop yourself right there. If you don't know something to be true, don't state it as fact! Do your research. Fill in the blanks with actual facts, not things you make up. You can't trust your intuition nor can you trust your memory.

Declinism

Have you ever found yourself shaking your head at youth and thinking, "This is it. Instagram is going to be the death of the future. When I was a kid, we didn't have Snapchat filters and Instagram and we were a lot happier."? When you say something like this, you are engaging in declinism, where you assume the past was better than the changing times of the present or future [13]. Sadly, you are probably mistaken. People maintain a fairly consistent level of happiness throughout generations and changes often don't contribute to the overall decline of humanity since people are incredibly adaptable.

Don't resist change just because it takes you out of your comfort zone. The most successful people are open and adaptable to change. Just because a change scares you does not mean it's bad. Investigate things a bit more and keep an open mind.

Nudging

You have a choice between two perfectly good apples. One has a nick on the skin, though, so you choose the other apple. This is nudging, where a small factor that doesn't really matter influences your decision [13]. It fits in with the decoy effect and framing.

While choosing an unblemished apple doesn't have much impact on your life, bigger choices based on nudging can certainly have a bigger impact. For instance, choosing to pay extra for a different color could cost you extra money for no good reason. Before making a decision, compare every attribute something has and then decide what really matters and what really doesn't. For instance, does the nicked apple really make it less valuable?

Anchoring

In one study, people were asked to estimate if less or more than sixty-five percent of African countries belong to the United Nations [13]. Most participants guessed close to sixty-five percent, despite the answer being one hundred percent. This is a good example of how an anchor can seriously interfere with your judgment.

Forcing Functions

This mental model is a trap when you pair it with anxiety. In a forcing function, something forces you to take action [13]. It can be awesome when you need that push to stop procrastinating and an impending deadline acts like a forcing function. It can be bad when you don't leave the house because your fear of getting injured forces you to stay inside. It can also be bad when your boss says you must do something one way, when a better way gets the same result.

When a big idea or rule makes you feel that you must do something, ask yourself, "Do I really need to do this?" Consider what will happen if you don't. Will you still be alive? Will you lose your job? Probably not.

Theory Of Constraints

This can be a great mental model to add to your toolbox. Find the single greatest thing holding you back and figure out how to work around it [13].

But it can be a trap when you think that something is

constraining you, when it's really not. Consider when you think that your office is causing you to perform bad work because you feel confined. Is the office the real reason behind your slump, or are you burned out? Or consider when you think you can't move because you don't have enough money. Don't just assume something is a constraint. Find ways to work around it and investigate other things that may be constraining you even more.

The Tragedy Of The Commons

The tragedy of the commons is where the short-term actions of one person have long-term consequences for everyone else [15]. When you run into any sort of problem with society or a community of people, your actions impact everyone. This is especially true in companies, where the decision of a higher-up not to give Christmas bonuses hurts everyone by withholding the resource of money. It can impact a family, when you must decide to move for a job and your kids and spouse have to uproot their lives.

It is imperative to never be selfish or make the one decision that seems "good enough." Rather, you want to think about how your decision impacts everyone, positively and negatively. Then decide to do the one thing that has the fewest negative consequences. If you are planning to cut Christmas bonuses, consider how people might feel and become disgruntled. For the good of the company, which is nothing without its workers, you should consider cutting costs somewhere else in order to incur fewer negative consequences.

Certainty Effect

Humans prefer absolutes and clear answers. Hence, it follows that many people fall into the mental trap of the certainty effect, where they assume something is more certain than it really is. In a study by Tversky and Kahneman, students were offered an insurance that cost fifty percent less, yet only covered fifty percent of claims [2]. Eighty percent of students refused the insurance because fifty percent was not an absolute. In another study, people were offered four cups of coffee for a reduced price or three cups with the last cup free [2]. While the amount of money spent on coffee balanced out to be the same in both options, people chose the latter option because a free cup of coffee was a more discernible, or certain, than the small discount on four cups.

This is why the math is always important. Before you commit to any decision based on your gut, actually crunch the numbers. Which option really saves you money or time or resources? Only the math will reveal the true answer. Your brain can't comprehend such minute concepts, so your intuition won't be able to make a good decision.

Framing

Look at these two phrases: "I had four dogs" or "I had one more than three dogs." Both phrases say the exact same thing. Yet the one emphasizing a gain – "more" – seems larger. Now consider these two: "You need to lose ten pounds" or "You need to fit into a size 4." They also say the same thing, but the last one doesn't talk about loss so it seems more attainable.

In framing, the way something is phrased in terms of gains or losses will influence your judgment [13]. But this is often fallacious, since the same thing is being said. When you make up your mind about something, take a moment to rephrase things several different ways, highlighting the good and the bad, the loss and the gain.

Time Discounting

This is where our good old friend instant gratification comes into play again [10]. You want something *now* rather than later, even if getting it later is actually more beneficial. Your perception of time blinds you. An example is a study, where elderly adults were given a choice of whether to pay a bill now or later. Most chose later, even though the same amount of money was being spent either way [16].

Again, this is where math comes in handy. When faced with a decision now or later, ask yourself if you can afford to pay for something now versus later. Then ask if the amount of money is the same. This can help you make a more balanced decision, not swayed by time.

Decoy Effect

A study on the decoy effect allowed subjects at a movie theater to get a small bucket of popcorn for three bucks or a large one for seven. Most people chose the cheaper one because they didn't want a large. However, when a decoy was thrown in offering a medium bucket for six dollars, people tended to choose the larger and more expensive bucket [13]. Wait, what?

The decoy effect makes no sense. Yet it influences your thinking. When you have three options, the middle or most incongruent one will influence your choice toward the lesser or greater value. It is important to focus on what you really want and need to make the best decision. Don't let a decoy get in the way.

So when buying popcorn, gauge how hungry you are and buy the bucket that best meets your needs. In more serious life decisions, be sure to pick the option that meets your needs instead of the one that "sounds good" or "seems good."

Deterring Of Small Decisions

Dining alone, you keep your meal cost small. Yet when you're splitting the bill with a buddy, you get the more expensive meal. While you are spending more money, something about the idea of splitting a bill makes you disregard that fact.

That is why you should always do the math, even if you think, "Oh, I can afford it!" Keep in mind that when you spend forty bucks on a dinner instead of sixteen, it is still forty bucks, whether you split the bill or not. Keep in mind that cash is the same as credit, even if your plastic card is less real to you than cash when you pay for items. Finally, keep in mind that when you spend sixteen dollars on something that is half off, you didn't save sixteen dollars, you spent sixteen dollars!

Sunk Cost Fallacy

When you want to hold onto something because you don't want to waste what you have already put into it, you are engaging in sunk cost fallacy [13]. This can really hurt you as you hold into a sinking stock or a failing marriage, continuing to put in effort that does not do any good.

It is always wise to take a look at the things in your life that are costing you time, money, or happiness. Ask, "Is it still worth it?" Don't hang onto something because of the effort you have put in the past. Rather, consider that effort good for the time being and then realize that times change. Be open to letting go of things that no longer serve you. You will have more resources, energy, and happiness for the things that really matter.

Survivorship Bias

How do you look at statistics? Do you research statistics in your favor, or all-around figures? Which figures do you value more, the positive ones that support your endeavors or the negative ones that do not?

If you're a new small business owner, you may model your business after a handful of businesses which have survived. Or you may use these other businesses to support your decision to use a certain business model. Sadly, you don't bother to take in the businesses with your model that have totally failed. This plays into confirmation bias, where you seek out information that agrees with what you think and dismiss the rest. You set yourself up for failure as a result.

You can see how dangerous this is. It is perhaps wiser to consider businesses that have failed and learn what *not* to do than to engage in survivorship bias. If you are going on a dangerous hike, learn about how many lives have been lost on the hike and how you can avoid the mistakes of those fallen hikers, for example.

Understanding and accepting risks helps you prepare for them. Blithely expecting life to just be peachy and looking at only the successful or the survivors will only set you up for failure.

Ostrich Effect

Don't be an ostrich. That's all I can say!

While your problems may scare or overwhelm you, they will not disappear on their own. You must do actual work to get rid of them. When you think, "This isn't right," don't just shrug it off. Investigate what is not right and how to make it right.

When you feel tempted to put something off for later, consider that it may only get worse later. This is a good motivation to not procrastinate on solving your problems.

Salience

A plane crash is more dramatic, even though the odds of dying in one are quite small. Yet driving a car is more commonplace, even though the odds of dying in a car crash are extremely high. Thus, you avoid flying but drive to work every day.

When you are weighing two jobs, one has the best benefits and salary and company culture. Yet the other is prominent and famous. You lean toward the latter option, even though it is not the best one for you, just because of salience.

When you feel inclined toward a decision, ask if it is really the best decision. Just because something seems great doesn't mean it is, especially if salience is at play. Look at all the factors and go with the option that is statistically less risky or more beneficial. Ignore drama and prominence, as those factors don't really matter in the end.

Recency

In this bias, you tend to think that the present will last forever. You don't anticipate likely changes. Like in the stock market, you may think that things will continue as they are currently, but anyone who knows the stock market knows that it will change. Not preparing yourself for changes is a dangerous move.

Before making a decision, consider past trends and future projections by different sources. Don't just look at the newest data, as that data is likely to change. If something is static, such as a certain market, then you can bet on little change, but still keep an eye on that market.

Pro-Innovation Bias

You get a new phone and you think it's the greatest thing in the world, so you overlook the few problems it has. When the phone is recalled, all of your friends are mad at you for making them buy it.

To avoid this issue, you must not let the innovation of some new, novel thing cloud your judgment. Instead, you want to take a few days or weeks to feel it out. Test the product or idea and see if it works. If you notice problems, attempt to rectify them.

I am confident that pro-innovation bias is why big tech companies like Apple will release very buggy versions of new technology, only to fix the bugs after customer complaints. They are so excited about their new features that they fail to adequately test the products for quality and identify bugs prior to release. This is obviously problematic and can cost them customers. They should be proof that taking your time to test something out is always ideal in the long run.

Placebo Effect

When you are given a sugar pill and told it will make you sleepy, sure enough, you feel sleepy. Your mind has an amazing ability to bend reality based on what it's told in the placebo effect [13]. But you can overpower your mind by considering what is actually real.

You can overcome the placebo effect by adjusting your beliefs. If you don't believe that something will work, it won't. If you do believe it, then it will.

Clustering Illusion

When you see a pattern in something random, you may think you're a genius. Chances are, however, you're just buying into the clustering illusion. Don't let movies like *Pi* convince you that there are patterns in everything. Even if there are, you probably won't ever be able to find them with your mind. The patterns are far too large and appear random. That's why you must not trust patterns you perceive, as chances are they are false.

A good example is when you infer a pattern between your work performance and the color you wear. That pattern is not likely true. You may have been in a productive mood while wearing green; the color green had nothing to do it with it at all. When you see this pattern, ask yourself how likely it is and do some research into colors and how they affect the brain. That way, you can let go of strange beliefs that simply don't hold water.

Chapter 4: Breaking Down Your Mental Models In Everyday Life

When it comes to real life, you use mental models constantly to save time and make snap decisions. Imagine the futile energy expense of deliberating for hours over what to eat – it doesn't serve you. But if you have a mental model that you want to eat clean, for example, you save time by picking healthier mealtime options.

While most mental models serve you in everyday life, others hurt you. Remember, mental models are imperfect time-saving methods that your mind employs in order to conserve energy. Also remember that mental models are built on your own perceptions and imagination, rather than logic and facts. Trusting mental models all of the time is thus a good way to make some bad decisions. If you tend to repeat a lot of the same mistakes or get into the same situations over and over, you are probably using bad mental models in everyday life. It is time to fix them and live your best life.

When You Use Narrow Thinking

Every day, you run into problems. You must judge the best solution. With narrow thinking, you continually limit yourself and hold onto the idea that things are black and white. You find yourself repeating the same mistakes, categorizing things the wrong way, and having to choose between two evils.

This may appear in your daily life as you get into arguments. You refuse to listen to anything anyone has to say on a subject. As a result, you are not exactly fun to talk to, at least about politics or whatever it is you are narrow-minded about. People avoid bringing up this subject at the dinner table because of how you are. To make people enjoy your company more, be open to other opinions and say, "We can agree to disagree."

Furthermore, stop insisting that you are always right. This can cause the dissolution of a relationship. Instead, think of how to find the *best* answer and be open to the fact that you are wrong. In a marital disagreement, being right is seldom helpful. What is the most reasonable solution that benefits both of you?

You may be narrow-minded in that you make decisions the way you always have. You avoid certain people because of preconceived notions about them and you avoid certain tasks because you disagree with them. Ask yourself if you may be wrong and consider broader evidence before each decision you contemplate.

When You Use Emotional Reasoning

Without a doubt, humans are inclined to use emotion in their judgment [17]. This can lead to flawed logic that is not based on reality, or it can cause you to make a decision that no longer makes sense once your mood shifts. Using logic instead of emotion is always key to any good decision.

If you are faced with a big decision and you are in a bad mood, ask for more time and hold off. Spend some time weighing the logical parts of a decision instead of making a snap judgment based on your mood in the moment. On the other hand, if you are in a great mood, slow down and consider the bad parts of a decision before you engage in optimistic bias. A good example is when you are offered a job. Instead of accepting it because you are happy to hear back from an employer, take a moment to see if this job is really right for you.

Don't Make Assumptions

Your spouse does not answer a text so you assume she's mad at you and you come home prepared for a fight. Your actions thus trigger a fight.

Your child doesn't want to talk about his day so you assume he had a bad day. You push him to tell you all about it. In reality, he is just in a hurry to hop on video games with his friends and your concern irritates him, leading to a fight.

You assume your boss wants you to call a client. You make the call and later your boss yells at you for doing something he didn't want you to do. By assuming you knew what your boss wanted, you screwed up.

In a final example, you assume your new neighbor is a bad person because he has a lot of tattoos. Thus, you act terse and rude toward him, which angers him. Your relationship becomes negative from the start. You never give him a chance to prove who he is.

Never take what you think you know as the truth. Always consider that your assumptions are wrong.

Before making a judgment, find out all of the facts. Ask your spouse is she is mad at you; ask your child if he had a bad day; take some time to get to know your neighbor. You can avoid a lot of strife if you refrain from acting on assumptions.

Chapter 5: Breaking Down Your Mental Models In Business

Mental models in business are quite harmful because you are attempting to predict and interpret the behavior of millions of consumers, the economy, and the competitors. Unless you clear your mind of entrapping mental models and attempt to think outside of the box, your organization will sink and your progress in the business world will be impeded. You positively must learn how to make good decisions with limited information.

How You Can Understand Complex Adaptive Systems

A complex adaptive system is a system that helps something evolve and change for survival in the face of complex and unpredictable problems [18]. It can be used to explain how organizations behave when faced with problems, such as economic slowdowns, unpredicted market changes, or competition. Being able to survive in the business world requires efficient complex adaptive systems, or else companies will fail [18].

The cool thing about complex adaptive systems is that they involve many agents and many disciplines. Any organization is comprised of hundreds or thousands of components. You've got different types of employees, equipment, protocol, and the like, and they all depend on each other for the organization to thrive. View your organization as a machine with many parts that work to achieve a unified result.

The main thing to realize is that a small change in one part of the organization can lead to huge changes throughout. Furthermore, since different parts of the organization can behave randomly, sometimes the movements of the organization can be unpredictable and effects can be hard to measure from small independent actions of different people.

It is important to remember that an organization will always attempt to go back to homeostasis, or sameness. If a change happens, the organization will struggle to rectify it, perhaps by making a new policy or firing a perceived troublemaker. To thrive in business, you must be willing to reach homeostasis by focusing on creativity and expanding into new realms. You must also be flexible and adaptive to change, since times change and a static company will eventually become obsolete. Finally, if something your company is doing is not working, the company is bound to fail. Recognize when things are not working well and propose a change from the top down.

How You Can Use These Systems In Business

A huge component of a complex adaptive system calls for creativity and thinking of alternative solutions when faced with problems. Think of Sprint and how they adapted to their image problem. Sprint knew that it had a bad reputation as not being as reliable as Verizon, so it decided to poach the "Can you hear me now?" guy and market themselves as being only two percent less reliable than Verizon. They also offered a free iPhone, which is a big incentive and works on the reciprocity principle [14]. This was a creative approach to affect a small change in their image, which in turn caused bigger change by making the company more successful.

These are examples of how creativity can help you overcome competition and image problems by adapting to the current trends and offering what competitors do in a slightly different way. But what about when you encounter problems with the economy or when your company products start to become obsolete?

A good example here would be Apple. Apple is more than happy to change and adapt with the times. As people want new technology, Apple stays ahead of the curve by rolling out some new tech product every year. They practically invented smartphones as we know them today and thus pushed tech trends themselves, giving themselves an advantage by being a leader in the industry.

When you feel that customers don't want what your company offers, change the product to meet the trends. Be open to changing with the times. Study what people say, post, and gripe about other products to create something that solves their problems. Furthermore, involve different disciplines. For example, you might be surprised what a physicist can do for a marketing company, but he might be able to offer some fresh insight into the rules of the world.

Make Yourself Better Mental Models

To make decisions that help rather than hinder business, use Occam's Razor, the less-is-more effect, and inversion.

Based on the principle of Occam's Razor, you know

that the simplest answer is often the truest one. You want to test the simple answer instead of taking it for granted, but you can almost always count on it being right.

With less is more thinking, studies have shown that people make better decisions with less information [19]. Why this is true is unknown, but it is possible to make great decisions based on the greatest probability of an outcome happening. You absolutely don't need to cloud your judgment with tons of extra details. Look at market trends, things that have worked in the past, things that have failed – and then go from there based on probability.

Inversion involves looking at a problem backward. For instance, if you are trying to figure out a marketing problem, your natural approach is to think about how your company can appeal to customers. If you invert it to think about how a customer wants to see your company, then you get more answers about how to market yourself.

Chapter 6: Removing Your Prejudice And Stereotypes

It is quite clear that our social systems are not perfect. While fixing our social systems is a worthy endeavor, I do not believe that you should feel overconfident in the difference that you make. Also, don't assume that your efforts will cause better than harm.

Every action has an intended reaction and an unintended one as well. Being prepared for the unintended is a bit like reading a crystal ball; it is beyond the skill of most people. But if you apply first principles thinking, first- and second-order thinking, and the information you learned from similar mistakes in your past, you can cover a few more bases. You should also avoid engaging in prejudices and stereotypes, which are both mental models that force your thinking into a narrow tunnel.

You Categorize People And Things

When we sort people into categories, it makes things easier. If someone falls into a good category, we can apply a mental model that allows us to trust said person. On the other hand, if someone falls into a bad category, we have a mental model that instructs us to avoid said person. The problem with having a few neat categories is that these categories fail to encompass all of the different people and social situations we encounter in life. Thus, we have very limited means of knowing how to deal with people. In addition, it is possible to sort people into incorrect categories.

Categorizing people is often the basis of prejudices. Racism is often taught in a "us versus them" form [20]. It is white people versus black people, for example, or citizens versus immigrants. The categories you learn from an early age influence you to make prejudiced choices against a certain group without taking the group's good qualities into account.

It is more ideal to avoid categorizing people and instead respond to their actions. Don't sort people into good and bad categories. Rather, determine behavior that is acceptable and that which is not to you. Then draw boundaries at unacceptable behavior. People cannot be categorized and treated the same, but behavior can.

You Should Avoid Stereotypes

Stereotyping is just a form of categorization where you make predictions about people or social situations based on the categories you sort people into. If you assume that someone is a thug based on his appearance, for instance, you instantly assume the way he acts, the type of music he likes, and even what he does for a living. When contrary evidence comes to light, you are surprised and you may engage in disconfirmation bias to restore the comfort in your mental model of stereotyping. Sadly, stereotyping causes you to miss the bigger picture and make predictions that are not accurate.

Just because two people belong to a group, such as a religious group or a racial group, does not mean that they are the same. Everyone has unique traits and ideals that make them different. Ditch the categorizing and narrow thinking that makes you stereotype and try to get to know each person at an individual level before you decide something about them.

Furthermore, it is important to let your own individuality help you avoid falling into stereotypes yourself. Many people believe that because they belong to a certain group, they must act, dress, and speak in certain ways. If that stereotype jars with who you are as a person, then don't play into it. Being your own person helps you avoid being categorized by others. For example, if you grew up in a rough part of a city and you want to become more successful, then you should not speak like everyone in your home neighborhood. Surprise people and prove yourself by learning how to speak eloquently and correctly.

Consider Society As A Complex Adaptive System

Society is typically arranged in a hierarchy, which governs the complex adaptive system that society forms [21]. Hierarchy helps mitigate crisis and confusion, but it can become problematic. Changing the hierarchy is the only way to bring about social change, but it is not always easy. Since upper levels of the hierarchy are often respected authorities, telling them to change is not an effective strategy. They can simply ignore you or tell you no.

Furthermore, most people respect the way things are and fear change, so even if people agree that social systems are broken, they still won't do anything about it. It can be hard to find allies for change.

More often than not, "the man in charge" is not to

blame for social practices or systems at all. He is simply upholding the status quo. Humans tend to operate on a series of norms that govern behavior, such as standing in line at a bank or holding doors open for people [21]. Without the guidance of a central control agent, people tend to find things that work and then others follow without question. To truly bring about social change, you must demonstrate a new norm and see if it catches on. People are resistant to it in a need to uphold the status quo, but sometimes very good new ideas take off.

Trying to take control of some things, such as social norms that people engage in independently of a central control agent, is almost always a bad idea [21]. People will not accept control over mundane and minute aspects of their lives. Trying to change the way people stand in line, for instance, probably won't work.

Therefore, it is best to never develop an exaggerated sense of control within society [21]. Even if you have a leadership position, you cannot finely control every link in the system. You must give people their autonomy and act as a guide or model rather than a dictator. People will respect your authority more and you will have more success this way. Model what you want to see happen – don't make it a law.

How Interconnectivity Endangers Systems

Research has found that our society is "near decomposability," meaning that most connections between people are not stable and society is bound to change at frequent intervals [21]. When the members of the system are too connected, they rely too heavily on these fragile connections and that creates conflict and impedes the speed of decisions [21]. Thus, autonomy is imperative for a society to run smoothly.

You must avoid depending too much on others when

making decisions. Independence is almost always ideal in decision-making and problem-solving. Involving too many people on a team at work is often disastrous, leading to conflict and miscommunication and a few people who don't pull their weight. The same goes for your everyday life, as you must make decisions for yourself without enlisting a huge number of opinions from others. The opinions of others will only cloud your judgment and make you more confused.

The Importance Of Using Your Creativity In Social Situations

Having a big toolbox helps you address more problems and decisions in social situations the right way, as you have more options to choose from. Being open-minded, getting all of the facts, and learning more broad social skills can help you exponentially in social situations.

It is helpful to experiment. If a certain method of

conflict resolution does not help in a certain scenario, it is time to move on to another. Be willing to admit when you are wrong and find an alternative solution. For example, in an argument with your spouse, you may find that stonewalling and walking away only makes your spouse angrier. To enjoy peace in your marriage, you can try a different approach, such as gently talking the issue out.

Chapter 7: Mental Maps In Science – Necessity Or Disruption?

Mental models are often harmful in science, since the purpose of science is to be objective and unbiased and interpret data as it is. Unfortunately, since humans must interpret data in some way, they often use biases and mental model traps to do so. This can obscure the real data and produce warped results.

Scientists are trained to avoid this problem, but sometimes human nature gets the best of them still. If you are in a scientific or engineering field, it can be helpful for you to learn about common traps and their problems in the sciences. Only when you free your mind of these traps can you be a truly unbiased scientist or engineer.

The Danger Of Using Confirmation Bias

So many scientific studies have been hurt by the confirmation bias [22]. When a scientist is after a certain result or bent on proving a hypothesis, he is bound to interpret facts that are favorable to his hypothesis and ignore the ones that are not. For science to be trustworthy and sound, however, this bias must be avoided at all costs.

A great example may be the blunders in forensic science committed by the Italian law enforcement in the Amanda Knox murder case. So determined to convict Knox, the police even misinterpreted DNA evidence and twisted circumstances of the case to frame her. The result was Amanda Knox was wrongfully convicted and imprisoned for four years. The problem here is obvious: you can't let a desired result make you twist the facts. You have to observe the facts as they are, even if they disprove your hypothesis.

Popular science is particularly guilty of flagrantly disregarding the facts [22]. The writer of a blog might hate eggs, so he focuses on studies that say eggs are bad and doesn't bother with studies that say they are good for you. Furthermore, pop science writers often fill in the blanks of dense scientific literature that they don't understand or draw their own hypotheses without testing them, both of which go firmly against the accuracy standards that science is firmly rooted upon.

You must remind yourself at all times that you could be wrong. Even a hypothesis that has been confirmed with one study can be disproved later on. Nothing is ever "proved" in science, only disproved. Therefore, you must recognize when you are assuming that something is right or that something "should" be a certain way. That helps you remove confirmation bias from your mind.

Also, be leery of popular science. It is always helpful to read the studies behind the literature. Articles that don't quote sources cannot be trusted, as they probably borrowed their content from other similar articles and did not bother to fact check and possibly lost things in translation. Sources like Wikipedia cannot be trusted because random people can submit incorrect facts and you read them before a moderator can delete them. Always check the references to Wikipedia claims and dismiss Wikipedia data should there be no corresponding reference.

Finally, avoid approaching a problem in science from a certain angle. With the help of a team or at least one other party, brainstorm a few possible scenarios and approaches. That way, you have a broader approach to the research and can accept results that contradict one hypothesis.

How You Can Have Good Mental Models In Science

When you break out of a mental model that restricts your ability to interpret data in a particular way to confirm a belief you hold, you are able to employ much more helpful mental models. Mental models drive science and scientists must have high-quality ones in place to perform good work.

The first good model is thinking outside of the box. When faced with how to confirm a hypothesis, scientists must come up with a research model that does not leave dependent and independent variables, measurability issues, or other such problems to mar the findings. While this is not always possible, thinking outside of the box can help you accomplish this goal. Furthermore, you must be open to accepting when a study is inaccurate and redoing it with a better design. In some cases, ethics may prevent certain types of research, so finding creative ways to conduct the research ethically is imperative to prevent a halt on the advancement of knowledge.

Questioning everything is another attribute of scientists. If you never take any rule as a given, you can poke holes in long-standing theories and make breakthroughs. Often, this type of research is highly objectionable in the scientific community, until years later when more research confirms the findings. Being willing to challenge accepted rules is the epicenter of science.

Scientists must always avoid the Dunning-Kruger Effect and instead employ a view that they don't know much about anything in reality. With this open-minded and humble viewpoint, scientists are able to free their minds of firm beliefs that can lead to confirmation bias.

A final great mental model is to use multiple disciplines at once. Maybe you are a geologist so your discipline helps you understand rocks, but to truly get a full picture of a natural phenomena, you also need a volcanologist, an ecologist, a meteorologist, a biologist, and so on and so forth. By using other disciplines, you gain a much greater depth of understanding of one thing. With just one discipline, you are only offered one tiny slice of the much bigger pie.

Chapter 8: How You Can Change Your Life: Liminal Thinking And Mental Models

Liminal thinking is the belief that by changing your thinking, you can change your life [23]. The great thing is, liminal thinking and mental models have a huge connection. You can use liminal thinking to restructure harmful mental models and get more mileage out of your problem-solving.

Liminal thinking states that beliefs are models that instruct you how to deal with the world. Beliefs create a shared world, such as in social beliefs and popular ideals, and change is only possible with a group effort. In addition, we fiercely defend our beliefs, even though we create them and therefore they may be flawed. As beliefs can create blind spots, we must act to change them. Some beliefs, called governing beliefs, form the basis of your identity and cannot be changed without restructuring your whole self; these can include things like ideas about your gender identity, your morality, your faith, and your ethnic and racial background. Other beliefs, such as the ones about how to communicate or how to handle dishonesty, can be changed and often do change on their own as you gain life experience.

Start With Identification

Your beliefs frame your entire reality. To bring about change, you must realize that your beliefs are not the end-all, be-all of existence. They are flexible. By accepting that your beliefs can be changed and a new reality is possible, you start to open the door to change [23].

Look at your life and identify the problematic areas. Maybe you have relationship troubles or financial troubles that never seem to go away, no matter how hard you try to fix them. Maybe you keep ending up with mentally abusive partners or you keep taking jobs that you hate.

Next, consider your beliefs about the exact problem. If you have repeated relationship problems, you might consider analyzing your beliefs and thoughts about relationships, partners, and how to communicate. Somewhere, you will locate a belief that seems to lead to the same bad results. That it is the mental model you must change to see change in your love life [23].

To make it simpler, you could look at a single time recently when things went wrong in your relationship. Your spouse requested that you leave the toilet seat down and it turned into a massive argument. Now, analyze your thoughts before, during, and after the argument. By doing this, you can see that you want to hold onto your independence, which made you resist your spouse's simple request because you don't want to be told how to live. This belief that you must have your independence is at odds with the need to make compromises for your spouse's comfort. You must decide which belief is more valuable – the belief that you need your independence or the belief that you want to be married to someone. If you want to be married more than you want your independence, you can work on changing that response; but if your independence matters more, maybe marriage is not for you yet.

Because most people don't want to be wrong, identifying the things you do incorrectly or even destructively can be quite painful. It takes a lack of pride and a courageous willingness to abandon the pillars you rely on to keep your life neat and tidy. When you accept that your beliefs are not actually reality, but just a model you have created of it, then you are able to get this courage and humility. Often, it is helpful to think of your beliefs as maps of life; sometimes, these maps are wrong and need to be corrected to lead you the right way.

How To Change Your Thinking

Changing your thinking takes practice. It does not happen overnight. Here are some tips on how to accomplish this change.

Disrupt Your Routine

When you are doing the same things over and over, you can enter a thinking tunnel that creates narrow-mindedness. By doing things a little differently, you suddenly use different parts of your brain and find a new way to do things. This can help you identify a new belief or way of doing things that works better.

Back to the example of your spouse asking you to leave the toilet seat down, normally you start a fight to preserve your independence and that never ends well. Now try disrupting that routine by responding differently. Think of several different ways to respond and try each one out. See which ones lead to conflict resolution and which ones lead to further trouble.

Ask Questions

"Should I really be doing this?" or "Is there another way to do this?" are two very powerful questions to ask yourself before you commit to any action (or inaction). Especially if your decisions have landed you in hot water before, asking yourself these two questions can help you pause and think.

You can go even deeper with more questions. "Why do I do this?" "How do I feel?" "Did I learn this behavior?" "Am I doing this because of something from my childhood?" You get the idea.

Be Aware Of A Lack Of Objectivity

When in the middle of a conflict, take a moment to imagine yourself in the other person's perspective. How does this person feel? What does he or she want? Why is he or she doing this?

When you do this, you can come up with very creative solutions that get you both what you want. You also make your opponent happier because you consider his or her feelings and needs. Normally, you don't consider the other person and keep fighting for what you want, which leaves no room for a solution that satisfies both of you.

Try Something New

It is so common to keep the status quo by doing the same things because that is how they have always been done. The problem is that you don't address things that are not working. Thus, you must ask, "Is there a better way of doing this?"

When you actually challenge the status quo, you make room for innovation and change. The United States is currently in a liminal period where long-held beliefs are being overturned, such as ones about gender identity, gay marriage, and abortion [23]. While it creates a lot of conflict, it also opens the door for new things and new experiences. You can also enter a liminal period by seeing where things you do are not working or where you can do things more efficiently.

Chapter 9: Cognitive Dissonance – An Enemy Inside Your Head

That discomfort you feel when your ideas are challenged, when your actions don't mesh with your beliefs, or when you are asked to do something you disagree with – that is cognitive dissonance [24]. The jarring sense that two ideas do not go together throws your brain into a state of frantic confusion. To make sense of reality again, your brain will usually adjust its beliefs or its behavior to reach a state of equilibrium again.

A good example is when you like two products a lot and you rate both highly. Yet when forced to choose between them, you make the choice and then rate the item you chose as higher, even though it is the exact same as the other. You did this because your brain is trying to convince itself that it made the right choice by saying one item is better than the other.

Another example is when you smoke and you know it

is bad for you. You dismiss studies saying that smoking is bad for your health, or you simply choose not to think about those studies. You use disconfirmation bias and the Ostrich Effect to keep your "consonance," or inner peace. People will use a number of denials, rationalizations, and biases to avoid cognitive dissonance.

Psychics supports the difficult concept that two diametrically opposed ideas can still both be true. Yet the human brain is not quite there. You can only hold one idea at a time; when you have more than one, cognitive dissonance occurs and you must change or favor one idea over the other.

People who crave consistency in life are much more prone to cognitive dissonance. Flexible people who are willing to let beliefs go are less affected by this phenomenon. Further, people who commit to a course of action are likely to "push" their beliefs to avoid second-guessing themselves and later regretting their choices. Admitting that a decision was poor is difficult for most people, which is why many people refuse to apologize for wrongdoing or change their actions when it is obvious that they should.

Is It Bad?

A cognitive dissonance is the way you lie to yourself. Such lies prevent you from accepting and acting on the real truth. This can certainly be bad.

But consider lies. Not all are "bad." A harmless white lie to make someone feel better can be a good thing to smooth over awkward social situations.

If a cognitive dissonance is small and harmless, then it is not something you need to worry about. But when it comes to bigger lies you tell yourself, such as "My marriage is good" when physical abuse is present, you really are putting yourself in harm's way just to keep consonance and avoid uncomfortable change in your life.

Really knowing yourself entails letting go of cognitive dissonance. To truly know yourself, you must stop lying. That can be liberating, but also painful. Most people are not willing to embrace themselves in such a raw, real way, where they cannot deny their mistakes, wrongdoings, and flaws. It is up to you if you are willing to do this.

Cognitive dissonance is almost always bad if it involves another person. Telling yourself that you love someone when you are not happy with him or her is an example of when lying to yourself can be harmful. You string someone along, trying to keep a relationship alive that is doomed to fail. You don't let the person go to find real love when necessary. This is just an example, but you can see that lying to yourself about other people is never a good idea.

Cognitive Dissonance And Your Personality

While everyone experiences cognitive dissonance, only certain personalities are prone to painful cognitive dissonance. In a study, introverts and extroverts were compared in their responses. They were asked questions and gave their opinions. Then they were told that the opinions of the group strongly contradicted their own [25]. Introverts were more likely to change their opinions to match the group's. Extroverts were more comfortable with the challenge to their own ideas.

Flexible, open-minded people were also less likely to experience this issue. If you are willing to accept several ideas and find the best one to match your needs or personal values, you will not experience the pain of cognitive dissonance.

Women are more prone to cognitive dissonance because they are torn between their rights and their prescribed roles in society. Often, they are conflicted about what is right because they are told so many different things.

To get over problematic cognitive dissonance, you can try to change your personality to be more extroverted and accepting and open-minded. Or you could try the tips in the next few sections. Personality change is seldom necessary or easy; but as you change your mental models, your personality will naturally change in a positive way as well.

Overcoming Your Inherited Ideas

Many of the ideas that cause cognitive dissonance are deeply rooted ones that you are unwilling to change. Often, these ideas were taught to you by family, peers, or even teachers at school. Such ideas founded a safe way for you to look at the world.

Overcoming these beliefs is only possible when you are willing to do so. You must see when an idea you hold poorly jives with the world. A constant state of cognitive dissonance suggests that you are holding onto a belief that the world routinely disproves. When you have to defend a belief and construct ways to keep believing it, then you have a belief that you must change.

When you feel the discomfort of cognitive dissonance, be sure to ask why. See what belief you are feeling conflicted over. Look at it honestly and ask yourself if it serves you anymore. If it does not, do research on other viewpoints and adopt a new one that seems to make more sense.

For example, if you insist that smoking is not that bad for you yet you keep seeing studies and your doctor keeps telling you to quit, go ahead and question the validity of your stance. Look into the studies and ask your doctor why he says what he says. What you see may convince you to finally accept that smoking is bad for your health. Then you can take steps to quit to fix the cognitive dissonance.

In some cases, changing your beliefs is not necessary. You should focus on changing your actions instead. If you always react to the news negatively and become stressed out, changing your beliefs won't help at all. Instead, you should stop watching the news.

Changing Your Mind...And Others' Minds

The confirmation bias, the disconfirmation bias, and the backfire effect are the means by which you guard your beliefs. Other people use these biases, too, which makes it quite difficult to change the minds of others. Even in the face of irrefutable evidence, people will deny or warp facts to stay in line with their beliefs.

One way to change someone's mind is to present the benefits of something to them, causing them to choose the option you want when they must ditch something to end the cognitive dissonance. For instance, someone may want to vote for a candidate, but you prove that he will benefit more from voting from another and his preferred candidate is actually a criminal. He feels dissonance that drives him to choose a candidate, so he chooses yours because he sees more benefit there. When you create an irresistible option, people will be willing to let go of their commitment and consistency for it [14].

You must also use recallability to make your ideas dramatic. If your ideas stand out to other people in easy recall, then people will go with your ideas. This is how you convince your boss to go with your presentation, for example.

You should never argue with a person and tell him that he is wrong. You instead must show him what is better. Being respectful avoids the defense mechanisms that make people cling to their beliefs harder.

When it comes to changing your own mind, you should always pick the mental tools and beliefs that seem to serve you best. By practicing this new line of thinking, it becomes habit over time. Be open-minded and willing to change if necessary. No one idea is ever right all of the time, so knowing this helps you be more open to finding the right attitude for the right situation.

It is said that addicts must hit rock bottom to change. Your rock bottom may be utter frustration that you can't seem to change your life. Let that act as a motivator to change your mental models and escape mental model traps.

The More You Know

A broader toolbox of mental skills can be a life-saver in overcoming the discomfort of cognitive dissonance. By having a wide variety of mental tools, you have more ways to address each situation. You can also find beliefs that are the most truthful for individual situations.

In all situations, try to think creatively. Ask lots of questions and brainstorm alternative solutions. Do not try to be right. It is often helpful to bring in different disciplines or outside opinions to get a well-rounded answer. Furthermore, you should look at situations from different angles, such as backward in inversion or from another person's perspective.

Conclusion

Mental models are pictures of expectations you have for the world. They make decisions a snap...until you realize that they are imperfect! Some mental models are wonderful while others create traps within your mind.

In this book, you learned about many mental model traps. But the number of mental model traps out there are too many to cover in a single book. The true takeaway is that when you feel that a decision is sound, you should step back for a moment and ask if you are overlooking something or playing into a bias. Nothing is ever certain in life, but when you are operating on incomplete information, you must get as much information as possible before committing to a life-changing decision.

Through examples, you learned ways that mental model traps can play into your life. But you will encounter mental model traps in all parts of life, in situations that vary greatly from the examples in this book. Again, realize that when you start to assume you have all of the facts or you know what your gut feels, it is time to think a little harder.

Don't rely on old ways of thinking and old decision-making strategies. Always think outside of the box and find new information, new strategies, new alternatives. You will never be perfect or right one hundred percent of the time, but by expanding your mental toolbox, you really can increase your odds of making good decisions.

Avoiding mental model traps is beneficial in your everyday life, your career, and your social life. Recognize traps when you start to fall into them and choose a new way of thinking. The result will be greater success and more happiness.

Don't put off making good decisions any longer. Start analyzing your thinking and identifying traps today.

You will be amazed at how much your life will improve.

Do you want to...

⇒ Stay up to date and hear first about new releases?

⇒ Get huge discounts and freebies?

⇒ Improve your thinking and have more success in life?

Sign up for our newsletter and get our thinking cheat sheet as a free bonus! Inside you'll find: 21 timeless thinking principles you need to know to upgrade your thinking and make smarter decisions (not knowing these may hinder you from having the success you'd like to have in life)

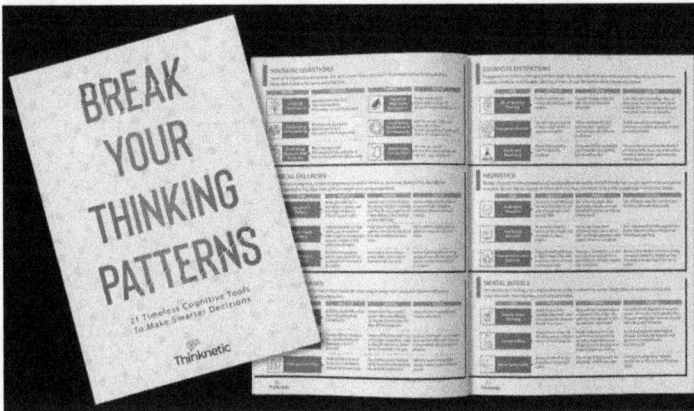

CLICK HERE TO DOWNLOAD FOR FREE!

Or go to www.thinknetic.net or
simply scan the code with your
camera

SCAN ME

References

1. Plous, Scott. The Psychology of Judgement and Decision Making. 1993. McGraw-Hill. ISBN: 978-0070504776.

2. Tversky, Amos & Kahneman, Daniel. Judgement Under Certainty: Biases and Heuristics. Oregon Research Institute. 1973. Retrieved from: https://apps.dtic.mil/dtic/tr/fulltext/u2/767426.pdf.

3. Gardner, Benjamin, et al. Making Health Habitual. British Journal of General Practice. 2012. Vol 62, No 605, pp. 664-666.

4. Baumersky, Roy & Tice, Dianne. Self-esteem and responses to success and failure: Subsequent performance and intrinsic motivation. Journal of Personality. 1985. DOI: https://doi.org/10.1111/j.1467-6494.1985.tb00376.x.

5. Xia, Tian, et al. Financial Literacy Overconfidence and Stock Market Participation. Social Indicators Research. Vol 119, No 3, pp. 1233-1245. 2014.

6. Buffett, Warren. A Colloquim with University of Nebraska-Lincoln Students. 1994. https://novelinvestor.com/investors/a-colloquium-with-university-of-nebraska-students/.

7. Inspiration. Teaching and Learning with Concept Maps. Retrieved from http://www.inspiration.com/visual-learning/concept-mapping.

8. Musk, Elon. Foundation 20 Interview with Elon Musk. Retrieved from https://www.youtube.com/watch?v=L-s_3b5fRd8.

9. Parrish, Shane. The Great Mental Models: General Thinking Concepts. ASIN: B07P79P8ST.

10. Mischel, Walter; Ebbesen, Ebbe B.; Raskoff Zeiss, Antonette (1972). "Cognitive and attentional mechanisms in delay of gratification". Journal of Personality and Social Psychology. 21 (2): 204–218. doi:10.1037/h0032198.

11. Bassok, M., & Novick, L. R. (2012). Problem solving. In K. J. Holyoak & R. G. Morrison (Eds.), OXFORD LIBRARY OF PSYCHOLOGY. THE OXFORD HANDBOOK OF THINKING AND REASONING (pp. 413-432). New York, NY, US: Oxford University Press.

12. What Is a Fishbone Diagram? Retrieved from https://asq.org/quality-resources/fishbone.

13. Nantchev, Adrian. 50 Cognitive Biases for an Unfair Advantage in Entrepreneurship. 2016. ASIN: B01M34BW42.

14. Cialdini, R. (2008). Influence, Science, and Practice, 5th Ed. Allyn and Bacon. ISBN-13: 978-0205609994.

15. Harden, Garrett. The Tragedy of the Commons. 1968. https://www.garretthardinsociety.org/articles/art _tragedy_of_the_commons.html.

16. Huffman, David, et al. Time Discounting and Economic Decision-Making in the Older

Population. ScienceDirect. 2017.
https://doi.org/10.1016/j.jeoa.2017.05.001.

17. Watson, J. B., & Rayner, R. (1920). Conditioned emotional reactions. Journal OF EXPERIMENTAL PSYCHOLOGY, 3(1), pp. 1–14.

18. Dooley, Kevin. (1997). A Complex Adaptative Systems Model of Organizational Change. Nonlinear Dynamics, Psychology, and Life Sciences, Vol 1, No 1.

19. Katsikopoulos, KV. The Less-Is-More Effect: Predictions and Tests. Judgement and Decision Making. Vol 5, No 4, pp. 244-257. 2010.

20. Cross, Beverly. Learning or Unlearning Racism. Theory into Practice. Vol 42, No 3, pp. 203-209. 2003.

21. Eidelson, Roy. (1997). Complex Adaptive Systems in the Behavior and Social Sciences. Review of General Psychology. Vol 1, No 1, pp. 42-71.

22. Byrd, Jon. Confirmation Bias, Ethics, and Mistakes in Forensics. Journal of Forensic Identification, Vol 56, No 4. 2006.

23. Gray, Dave. Liminal Thinking: Create the Change You Want by Changing Your Thinking. 2017. ISBN-13: 978-1538407189.

24. Festinger, Leon. A Theory of Cognitive Dissonance. 1957. ISBN-13: 978-0804709118.

25. Matz, D.C. Hofstedt, P.M. & Wood, W. (2008). Extraversion as a moderator of the cognitive dissonance associated with disagreement. PERSONALITY AND INDIVIDUAL DIFFERENCES, 45(5), 401-405.

Disclaimer

The information contained in this book and its components, is meant to serve as a comprehensive collection of strategies that the author of this book has done research about. Summaries, strategies, tips and tricks are only recommendations by the author, and reading this book will not guarantee that one's results will exactly mirror the author's results.

The author of this book has made all reasonable efforts to provide current and accurate information for the readers of this book. The author and its associates will not be held liable for any unintentional errors or omissions that may be found.

The material in the book may include information by third parties. Third party materials comprise of opinions expressed by their owners. As such, the author of this book does not assume responsibility or liability for any third party material or opinions.

The publication of third party material does not constitute the author's guarantee of any information, products, services, or opinions contained within third party material. Use of third party material does not guarantee that your results will mirror our results. Publication of such third party material is simply a recommendation and expression of the author's own opinion of that material.

Whether because of the progression of the Internet, or the unforeseen changes in company policy and editorial submission guidelines, what is stated as fact at the time of this writing may become outdated or inapplicable later.

written expressed and signed permission from the author.

CPSIA information can be obtained
at www.ICGtesting.com
Printed in the USA
LVHW031414190421
684904LV00019B/709

9 781698 053301